ROUGHSTOCK SONNETS

Barb,
It's so pleasing that
you're a fan of this work.
Enjoy it and have fun,
all my best!
Barb

D1476128

Sitting Pretty

ROUGHSTOCK SONNETS

Poems by
PAUL ZARZYSKI

Photographs by
BARBARA VAN CLEVE

Introduction by
JAY DUSARD

THE LOWELL PRESS / KANSAS CITY

ACKNOWLEDGMENTS

The author and publisher express their thanks to the following publications in which poems from this book first appeared.

CutBank: "Retiring Ol' Gray"

Elkhorn Review: "How the Lord Throwed-In with Mom to Make Me Quit the Broncs," "Rodeo-Road Founder: Highway Horseplay," "The Comeback," "April Showers"

Northern Lights: "Staircase"

Poetry: "Measuring"

A number of these poems also appeared in two earlier collections:

Call Me Lucky—a chapbook from Confluence Press, Lewis-Clark State College, Lewiston, Idaho, 1981.

The Make-Up of Ice—The University of Georgia Press, Athens, Georgia, 1984.

Special thanks to Elizabeth Dear, who sparked the idea to partner-up these poems and photographs—for her creative savvy along the book's trail.

Library of Congress Cataloging in Publication Data

Zarzyski, Paul.
Roughstock sonnets / poems by Paul Zarzyski; photographs by Barbara Van Cleve; introduction by Jay Dusard.
p. cm.
ISBN 0-932845-35-5: $10.00
1. Cowboys—Poetry.
2. Ranch life—Poetry.
I. Van Cleve, Barbara, 1935-
II. Title.
PS3576.A77R68 1989
811'.54—dc20 89-14513 CIP

Printed in the United States of America
by The Lowell Press of Kansas City, Missouri.

To all the buckers
who've taken us to the tooter
or taught us humility.
And in memory of Spike Van Cleve, Horseback Man,
and Ben Herzog, Roughstock Rider—
God Bless them with big-hearted draws.

Filly Chasing

CONTENTS

Ground Blizzard

INTRODUCTION

OLD CHEYENNE

The band would play the anthem, and
The clowns fell down in jest.
All the people saw again
The winning of the West.

Ian Tyson

All it takes is eight seconds—to win it (or lose it) on a rodeo bronc or bull. In the same amount of time it takes a cheetah to race one-eighth of a mile of Serengeti Plain, or a human to lose consciousness once the blood supply to the brain is interrupted, a roughstock rider replays the whole scene, this manifest destiny in microcosm, for the crowd and for himself. For contestant and spectator alike, the rodeo arena is the Great American Desert, and the chute-gate or scoreline is the Hundredth Meridian.

Industry is not known for spawning major sports, but American rodeo and its Mexican counterpart, *charreria,* are clearly derived from the range cattle business. Rodeo is the theme that brings together the work of two artists and friends: Paul Zarzyski, a wrangler of words, who came west from the iron ore district of northernmost Wisconsin, and Barbara Van Cleve, a catcher of shadows, whose Montana ranching-family roots are truly those of the cowboy sport. Having Paul's poems and Barb's photographs together in this book is like owning a pen full of top-notch buckers. Herein we've got something equivalent to Staircase, Willie Rock, Lonewolf, Moonshine, Applejack, Creamo, Blue-Tail Fly, Linger's Strawberry and Kesler's Three Bars, ready and waiting behind the chutes.

"Her Levis, so tight I can read the dates on dimes in her hip pocket." Fifteen words make up a picture that's supposed to be worth a thousand of them little boogers. That's what I like about my bronc-ridin' friend Zarzyski ("rhymes with whiskey"); he's an economical writer, and extremely visual ("pigtails braided like bronc reins"). And touching: "It's bad and good some cowboys don't know tears from sweat. I folded both between fringes of your chaps," he writes about a rodeo partner who "took the ambulance, like a cab, front seat to Emergency."

Paul can regale you. At cowboy poetry gatherings, I've been a part of audiences dazzled and drooling over his gourmet menu of pies, and collectively cracked-up concerning "eight juicy monsoon seconds" spent on a bronco mare called April Showers.

I'm glad Barbie Van Cleve takes her camera to lots of rodeos and packs the cussed thing when she's horseback on her home range in south central Montana. If she didn't, we wouldn't get to see a saddle bronc rider glowing like an angel "sitting pretty" on a baldfaced outlaw, or another angelic twister, "in the money" and floating down from on high. Or the cowboy numbered Coors 309, bucked off but still hung in the rigging, who must be thinking that Hell ain't a hundred yards away. Or her savvy friend Polly, who has cranked a few dallies of her rosary around the saddlehorn, thus invoking her God at the precise spot where so many cowboy wrecks have occurred—the old apple, the fulcrum of the West, where both critters and fingers are harvested by the score.

Barb takes us beyond arenas and pens onto the grassy foothill slopes of the Crazies to gather a string of half-wild horses in "Filly Chasing." One of our pardners on this circle is "The Range Rider," a quintessential portrait of human, horse and land. The modest size of this book doesn't begin to do justice to "Noon Break." You really need to walk into the Andrew Smith Gallery in Santa Fe sometime and behold a framed original print of this, nearly four feet high. Now, that'll transport you to Big Sky Country.

Paul Zarzyski came out of the chute on his first bareback horse at Flint Creek Valley Days in Philipsburg, Montana, fifteen years ago. He's been rodeoing ever since, and writing poetry about the horses, the hands, the hallucinations, triumph, terror, love and loss. He can put you right there— "I call for the gate, hinges shriek, sand hisses against the chutes with every kick"—and bring on the memories.

My own rodeo initiation took place in Ft. Smith, Arkansas, when the Army had me temporarily assigned at nearby Fort Chaffee, in the spring of

1963. A local stock contractor needed to audition some bucking horse prospects, so he put out the word for riders to assemble one Sunday afternoon at the rodeo arena. Being male, ambulatory, and in possession of a bareback riggin' were the only requirements, so even this greenhorn passed muster. No entry fee, no prize money, three head per customer.

From the middle of bronc number one, I zeroed in on his ears and nodded my face. Sorrelly made a quick sashay to the left, and I plummeted down between his feet. I rolled into a ball to avoid the massive, whizzing, untrimmed hooves as he bucked over me into the arena. Farted off in the chute. Left in a heap behind my Gateway to the West.

"Are you sure you want to go through with this, kid?" sighed Mister Stock Contractor from somewhere up above.

"Yes sir. I'll do better on the next one."

By the time I came around in the rotation again, my chagrin was transformed into resolve. Numero dos was a dun, and I was ready. I rared back, asked for him, and turned on the spur-lick I had perfected on a couple of logging mules one day near Fort Polk, Louisiana. In perfect rhythm and way down the arena, here I was, winnin' the West and makin' it look plumb easy. Then, my zebra dun ducked off to the right, and yours truly kept going straight, hearing the splat just before the eight-second horn.

From down low again, I began to study the surface of the arena, marveling at how its slablike precision had scarcely been defiled by the once-over of tractor and disk. I felt myself being hoisted upwards by my armpits and transported back uprange. The cowboy on the right was four feet wide and all muscle; the guy on the left was smaller and asked if he could have my third bronc.

"No!"

Bronco three was a paint, and I was hurtin'. What I perfected on this go-round was a relatively soft landing, at four, maybe five, seconds into the mission.

The warm flush I felt as I hauled my carcass into the white GMC pickup that would soon take me irretrievably westward emanated from much more than a considerably bruised left gluteus. Before the Army cut me loose from Fort Polk, I entered the bareback riding at DeRidder and

Hineston, where both times I was bedded down in soft Louisiana mud well before the tooter. End of career. The glow diminished quickly, but there's a little warm spot left, somewhere between myth and memory.

About ten years ago, I spotted a book on a library shelf that turned out to be a treasure. By the second chapter of *40 Years' Gatherin's,* I knew that I absolutely had to meet the man who wrote it—one Spike Van Cleve. While on the road in 1981 photographing working cowboys from British Columbia to Chihuahua, I was able to trail up this Montana rancher and man of letters. Spike liked what I was up to and said he hoped I was doing a book of my cowboy portraits. It turned out that I was, and I'm delighted that my picture of him is a part of it.

When I was at Spike's, he showed me a photograph that had the mood and graphic power of a Frederic Remington snowstorm painting. "My daughter Barbie shot this during a ground blizzard that caught us while we were out huntin'," he explained. "I'm sittin' there on my horse, freezin', and wishin' she'd put her camera up so we could get our outfit the hell out of there."

I met Barbara around the time of Spike's death in 1982. We've been friends ever since, and have more recently become good friends of Mr. Zarzyski. Paul told me that for many years he's carried a copy of *40 Years' Gatherin's* in his war bag. He never had the pleasure of knowing Spike, but he wrote some lines for other ranching friends that could have just as readily been about Spike and Barbie:

> The West before wire
> still rides the lineage of this family ranch
> where broncs, pastured with the bridlewise,
> fashion a soft backdrop for lovers
> of horses—like father, like daughter—
> blue-ribboned in their Wind River embrace.

It's time to nod for the gate on this collection of words and pictures. Outside!
Let 'er buck!

Jay Dusard
Prescott, Arizona, September, 1989

"I like 'em," said the Pecos Kid, "for an outlaw horse
is usually gamer than a gentle one. I've rode the rough
string an' been a-snappin' broncs since I was old enough
to make a hand. An' a outlaw has always interested me
a heap more than a gentle horse. For when you find a outlaw horse that's really game he's just about the gamest
thing I know."

Ross Santee–
from "The Rough String"
(Men and Horses)

These twisters of to-day are made of the same leather
as the old-time ones. It ain't their fault that the
country's fenced an' most of the cows are wearin' bells.

Charles M. Russell–
from "Bronc Twisters"
(Trails Plowed Under)

… with the bucking horse, his only training is to be
on his native western range where over six months out of
a year he has nothing to do but graze, wax fat, hold his
wiry strength and hatch out more ways of bucking his rider
off. … But when the grass matures and is full of hardening
nourishment, he sheds off slick and the tough sparkle is in
his eye when he's loaded in the box car. Then grain and good hay
fed to him, and he's very ready, with every muscle
twitching and aching to bust a cowboy.

Will James–
from "The Bucking Horse"
(Horses I Have Known)

The Range Rider

ZARZYSKI MEETS THE
COPENHAGEN ANGEL

Her Levis, so tight
I can read the dates on dimes
in her hip pocket. Miles City,
a rodeo Saturday night.
She smiles from a corner bar stool,
her taut lower lip, white and puffed,
pigtails braided like bronc reins.
She leads the circuit, chasing cans,
a barrel racer in love with her horse,
her snuff, and a 16 second run.
We dance close to LeDoux's "Daydream Cowboy."
I'm Zarzyski, rhymes with whiskey,
I tell her—a lover, a fighter,
a Polish bareback bronc rider.
And these Copenhagen kisses jump and kick
higher than ol' Moonshine, himself.

FOR DEBBIE MOORE

How the Lord Throwed-In with Mom
To Make Me Quit the Broncs

Was my mother sayin' rosaries day and night
—beads coiled 'round each mitt—
that compelled the Lord to heed her prayers,
if He built this world in seven days
He could dang sure make me quit.

So first God hires on this angel,
a thief, a rustler, 'fore he come reborn,
to filch my warbag from the pickup cab—
"no gear, too broke to buy it new," God thought,
"**that'll** ear him down and leave him shorn."

Now I got no insurance on my life,
my health, my house, or half-ton Ford,
so when State Farm rushed that check
—full coverage for my losses—
you might say, it **surprised** the Lord!

Inside a week, I'm back a scratchin'
with riggin', hooks, rosin, chaps, and glove,
while God, studyin' hard his notes
on Rodeo—"How to break an addict"—
concocts plan B there up above.

"I'll hang him up," He figures, "spook him good,
have Kesler's Three Bars stomp his lights,
pop his stubborn pumpkin off arena posts
till he's floppin' like a neck-wrung chicken—
that'll squelch his fight!"

Now spurrin' bares is a bunch of fun
when yer gettin' holts and packin' extra luck,
but when yer hung, yer riggin's slipped,
and yer downstairs, it's a lot like slapshot
hockey—yer noggin plays the puck.

That mare rag-dolled me 'round the 'rena
left me caked with lather, blood, and dirt,
and yeah, I took some stitchin' up,
but even worse, my ridin' arm's much longer now—
it's a ***bitch*** to tailor me a shirt!

I'll hand it to the Lord on this one,
He come close to sourin' me for good,
but "close" don't count for nothin'
'cept in pitchin' hand grenades and horseshoes—
next day, I enters every rodeo I could.

When plans C thru V don't work no better
and the Almighty's runnin' shy of rope,
He savvies **W**, for Woman, "I'll make
that twister fall so hard in love and lust..."
she'd make me hang em up, He hoped!

Oh, she was the prettiest filly God give teeth
—next to her, Bo Derek scored a 2—
and I quit everything she asked,
from snoose, to hootch, to cussin' rank,
but no, not buckers, no matter how she'd coo.

So finally mom stopped prayin', and God's relieved
'cause He run out of plans with Z,
ol' Three Bars, she's retired, my gal's run off,
and you know, I'll be go-to-hell
if everyone ain't up and quit, ***but me!***

After the Calving

Running Before the Storm

Escorting Grammy to the Potluck Rocky Mountain Oyster Feed at Bowman's Corner

Lean Ray Krone bellers through a fat cumulus
cloud of Rum-Soaked Wagonmaster Conestoga
Stogie smoke he blows across the room,
"They travel in 2's, so better eat them even
boys, or kiss good luck good-bye for good."

Tonight the calf nuts, beer batter-dipped
by the hundreds, come heaped
and steaming on 2-by-3 foot trays
from the kitchen—deep-fat fryers
crackling like irons searing hide.

And each family, ranching Augusta
Flat Creek country, brings its own brand
of sourdough hardrolls, beans, gelatins,
slaws and sauces, custard and mincemeat
pies to partner-up to the main chuck.

At the bar, a puncher grabs a cow-
poxed handful—7 of the little buggers—
feeding them like pistachios
from palm to pinch fingers to flick-
of-the-wrist toss on target.

Grammy, a spring filly at 86, sips
a whiskey-ditch in one hand, scoops
the crispy nuggets to her platter
with the other, forks a couple
and goes on talking Hereford bulls.

And me, a real greenhorn to this cowboy
caviar—I take to them like a pup
to a hoof paring, a porky
to a lathered saddle, a packrat
to a snoosebox filled with silver rivets.

I skip the trimmings, save every cubic inch
of plate and belly for these kernels,
tender nubbins I chew and chew till the last
pair, left for luck, nuzzle on the tray
like a skylined brace of round bales.

A cattleland Saturday grand time with Grammy
is chowing down on prairie pecans, then driving
the dark-as-the-inside-of-a-cow grangehall
trail home to dream heifer-fat, bull-necked
happy dreams all night long in my Sunday boots.

FOR ETHEL "GRAMMY" BEAN

Noon Break

Retiring Ol' Gray

"Tailor-made," we'd say
each time the chutegate cracked
        and she'd buck honest—
a jump-'n'-kick rocking-chair
        bronc, not a "dirty" in her,
not a single swoop
        or duck: "no mallards"
we'd laugh. That campaigner
        taught us heart, those moments
she'd hang high
        enough for us to dream
fancy filigree with ruby
        inlays on the sun—the silver
buckle to win Cheyenne, like heaven,
        "Daddy of 'em All."

I'll always crave and miss
her acrobatic kick
        to kiss the earth,
the way she'd break in two,
        come up again for air
and float: back to back,
        we'd take wing, my high
spurring stroke lifting
        and lifting her, from horizon
to horizon—"The Bronco Pegasus"
        soaring to love
every inch of sky—rainbowing
        and high rolling for the clouds
going stark-raving
        wild in a crowd.

For Ralph Beer & Jake Woirhaye

PARTNER

As you hit ground off Staircase,
number 12, at the state fair
rodeo in Great Falls, it was hard
to hear vertebrae cracking
above the murmur of ten thousand
hometown hearts. You cowboyed-up
and hid your grimace deep,
walked out of the arena,
stubborn, on sheer pain
and took the ambulance, like a cab,
front seat to Emergency.

Tonight, drunk on Tanqueray,
we vow never again
to mention "broken neck." Instead
we talk tough broncs, big shows
we'll hit down south, and hunting ducks
come fall. We straggle home,
moon-struck, to the squawk of geese—
a V of snows crisscrossing
and circling the city—screwed-up,
you say, when streetlight glimmer
throws them off plumb.

When my bronc stomped
down the alleyway that night,
I knew down deep our bones and hearts
were made to break a lot
easier than we'd believe. I felt
your arm go numb in mine,
took the gate, weak-kneed, and spurred
with only half the try. It's bad
and good some cowboys don't know tears
from sweat. I folded both
between fringes of your chaps,
packed your riggin' sack neat
as you'd have, and wandered
punch-drunk lost, afraid
into the maze of parking lot.

What's done is done, I know,
but once I killed
at least a dozen singles
in a season, without thinking
how they partner-up for life
and death, how the odd ones
flocking south
survive that first long go alone.

FOR KIM ZUPAN

Polly's Dally

Toppin' Off a Green One

MATCHED PAIRS

        Was it the boot-cut Wranglers
you wore that night
        in Butte, those copper rivets
glimmering from the hip—eyes
        out of nowhere
on my lonely stretch of road? Something
        strong caught me a moment
off guard. I forgot my only love—
        rodeo—forgot good broncs and worst
pain I've had to stand, tailbone
        just cracked on Willie Rock
in the first go. We danced
        a cowboy waltz, holding
hands, moving smooth
        as if harnessed
together since colts.

        Outside Augusta, I sleep upstairs
buried eyeball-deep in the feather bed,
        quilts, and wool blankets woven
on Grammy's ranch. Flat Creek wind
        rumbles above mountain runoff
and the mothball smell lingers
        in this oak room closed to heat. Sleep deep

and you'll still hear, clean through wind,
        the new-branded calves
bawling to mother-up. Just smell
        that sage mixed with manure,
leather, denim and horse
        drifting from scattered boots
and jeans. Feel spirited
        as newlyweds the first time
together here, their faces
        warmed by silver
breath you can see
        melting into this beautiful dark.

Rough Stock

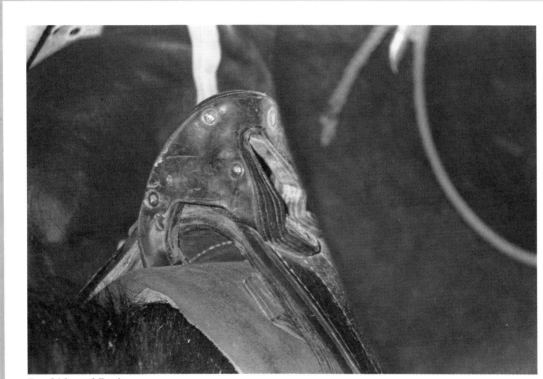

Rawhide and Rosin

Rodeo-Road Founder:
Highway Horseplay

Say horses were elk, and elk
horses: eyes around every elkshoe
curve would pack more weight, spook me
worse, and I'd be glued to the wheel, pulling
leather all night long, from Alberta, to Cranbrook
B.C., Sandpoint, Coeur d'Alene … after 8
hang-and-rattle seconds—spur to antler—
locking horns with a bucking wapiti.

Say elk were horses, and horses
elk: it's a long, hard haul after all but 1
of your 9 lives flash before your eyes
aboard a bugling cayuse, especially
when you draw old Velvet Double 7,
triple rank, his royal head of ivory
tines stabbing, battering you
half to death and senseless.

Say horses were elk, and elk
horses: caution
sign language would change in silhouette
and mustang eyes would shift
at different gaits from borrow pits
to the center of your lane. Daybreak,
you'd see compact cars, not ungulates
chassis-up and driving magpies mad.

Say elk were horses, and horses
elk: you'll say anything, won't you,
you knee-jerkin', suicide-circuit-
chasin' maniac of a loon—any singsong
screwball thing to stay alive when you're dead
tired, gassin' and mashin' it,
gettin' your holts and yodelin' down the road
rodeo to rodeo to rodeodeodeo …

FOR INSANE-WAYNE, TNT, LLOYD,
TERRY, STEVE, & LITTLE JOE

Chute Ballet

One on One

Crystal

Martini McRae & Whiskey Zarzyski:
A Brace of Blackjack Aces

Three mush-hearted dealers changed careers
'cause they couldn't gut the cruelty and the guilt.
The pit boss's shotglass-hard eyes broke to tears
watching, wrinkle-by-wrinkle, 2 cowpoke poker faces wilt.

Laughter in the rafters, the automated cameras convulsed
when walleyed Wally, holding 20, took a hit,
dealer showing 7. I heard his drumrolling pulse
above Mike Korn's cackling, caterwauling fit.

Me and Wally, we couldn't savvy what's the joke,
what's funny 'bout some palooka totin' off our loot
fast as stackin' bales—us goin' for broke
and him lathered through his pin-striped suit.

Shy on brain, but extra-extralong on sand and brawn,
we'd double-down on 3's or 5's and blow it.
But get pitched off, climb right back on—
"more chips! more drinks!" for the Marlboro bard & Polack poet.

We squandered all our gatherin's, includin' riggin' sack
and Rocker Six—wouldn't let us bet our poetry—
but then we sobered- and tallied-up, and lookin' back
we figured only winners drank all night "for free."

But poor McRae, still mutters something 'bout bad dreams,
asked why he's bruised and wearin' shades on rainy days.
He jolts in sleep, wife Ruth will vouch, and screams
"Hit me! Hit me! Hit me!" And she, wholeheartedly, obeys.

To all the Elko Gathering Cowboy Poets and Fans

All This Way for the Short Ride

After grand entry cavalcade of flags,
Star-Spangled Banner, stagecoach figure 8's
in a jangle of singletrees, after trick riders
sequined in tights, clowns in loud getups,
queens sashed pink or chartreuse
in silk—after the fanfare—the domed
rodeo arena goes lights-out
black: stark silent
prayer for a cowboy crushed by a ton
of crossbred Brahma.
                        What went wrong—
too much heart behind a high kick,
both horns hooking earth, the bull vaulting
a half-somersault to its back—
each witness recounts with the same
gruesome note: the wife
stunned in a bleacher seat
and pregnant with their fourth. In this dark
behind the chutes, I strain to picture,
through the melee of win with loss,
details of a classic ride—body curled
fetal to the riggin', knees up,
every spur stroke in perfect sync,
chin tucked snug. In this dark,
I rub the thick neck of my bronc, his pulse
rampant in this sudden night
and lull. I know the instant
that bull's flanks tipped beyond
return, how the child inside

fought with his mother for air
and hope, his heart with hers
pumping in pandemonium—in shock,
how she maundered in the arena
to gather her husband's bullrope and hat, bells
clanking to the murmur of crowd
and siren's mewl.
                    The child learned early
through pain the amnion could not protect him from,
through capillaries of the placenta, the sheer
peril of living with a passion
that shatters all at once
from infinitesimal fractures
in time. It's impossible, when dust
settling to the backs of large animals
makes a racket you can't think in,
impossible to conceive that pure fear,
whether measured in degrees of cold
or heat, can both freeze
and incinerate so much
in mere seconds. When I nod
and they throw this gate open to the same
gravity, the same 8 ticks
of the clock, number 244 and I
will blow for better or worse
from this chute—flesh and destiny up
for grabs, a bride's bouquet
pitched blind.

—IN MEMORY OF JOE LEAR

Before the Anthem

Crack 'er Back, Slide and Ride

APRIL SHOWERS

Most broncs I've rode were satisfied to spite you with a fart,
an echo to every pair of holes they'd punch through air.
But one crude pony throwed its kidneys, as well as heart,
into eight juicy monsoon seconds, epitomizing
how a stud or gelding aims more civil than a mare.

She was owned by howling broncman, old Bob Schall,
whose faintest whisper ball-peen hammered mirrors.
No doubt, he salted down her feed, kept her in a private stall,
doctored-up her water with a jug of diuretics,
'cause she'd let blow like someone holding back a hundred beers.

I swore she'd waterlog herself from show to show—
compared to April, Yellowstone's Old Faithful was a squirt.
With every jump she'd let that hydrant gusher go,
she'd drench her tail, pistol-whip you blind,
leave you looking jaundiced, make you burn your shirt.

The rulebook adamantly states you **got** to wear a hat,
and me, I'm partial, even in the heat, to beaver felt.
My Resistol resisted scours, gumbo, blood, and buzzard scat—
even soaked and shaped it once with rotgut rye—
but April's frothy acid sopping made the damn thing melt.

Funniest, though, was when some rookie'd pluck her from the draw—
as he'd size her up between catchpen rails, she'd nicker.
"She ain't rank, is she?" he'd beg us all to tell him **"nawww,"**
but finally, what burst our briskets was his face
bewildered by the flankman wearing waders and a slicker.

But you'd never turn Miss April out—she was tailor-made,
a skosh easier to track than, say, Sonny Linger's roan.
Sacrifice a little pride and hygiene, you'd get paid,
and learn what virtues lie in celibacy
plus solitude, as you'd go home or down the road alone.

April Showers brought you **no** May flowers—**NOR** a pick-up man!
She'd send you retching, reeking, sloshing to the nearest trough.
Win or lose, a swarm of flies was still your only fan,
and though she'd seldom spill a twister pitching
that sluicetail cayuse sure did **piss** some good ones off.

**FOR DON & DOUG, TUDO, LUCKY,
& WILD BILL STOCKTON**

FINALE

The iron drives this bay mare
crazy from chute 8, rowels zinging
like thumbnail-size flies
in fever heat, that sudden bite
and ring behind her ears
again and again, spurring every jump
and kick. She buries her head
blind between her knees,
hits the fence head-on,
wire mesh heaving. Her neck
snaps above the withers
where the rider feels life go
in one quick explosion of dust.
Mesh collapses like lung wall
on that last long breath. She tumbles
and shakes, the grandstand
stone-still, the cowboy pinned,
his face to her muzzle—hard
grimace to petrified stare.
And through that deep purple spectrum
end of pain, her nostrils
blossom pink and renegade
as wild rose, a single
springtime applause
in a graveyard of rimrock.

FOR MARDY AND WAYNE

CUTTING THE EASTER COLT

      This saddlebag surgeon readies his tools
like a Monsignor prepares
      for communion. Holy day or not,
nothing's sacrilegious
      when the moon comes
ripe, the disinfectant fumes
      stunning us hard as incense
at high mass. We lead
      the stud, procession-like, into the corral,
scotch-hobble and throw him
      fast with cotton ropes, then watch
this wrangler/pastor/sawbones—all-
      arounder—move his 55 years of heart
and savvy, lickety-split
      amid thrashing hooves
to lash all 4 together
      at the pasterns. He swashes
the scrotum, a glistening lobed
      world, delicate and thin-veined—perfect
contrast to his saddlemaker hands,
      fingers braided like rawhide bosals,
his knuckles the thick heel knots.
      With knife honed to a featheredge,
he makes the incision and probes
      until he hunts both down,
an Easter egg apiece for the blue
      heeler pups, their anxious panting
reflected in the gold
      chalice of the gelding's eye.

FOR EARL STEWART

Scratchin' High

Outside!

STAIRCASE

How can lovers of buckers lament
a favorite bronc down
and dying on timberline range
we glass for elk—meadow
he's pawed to a raw circle
around him like mool. What can we say
under this scant angle of Montana
half-moon, when we wish the whole
universe would grieve
for one rodeo star, throwing all
his heart into each roll
and futile lunge for all fours—
first stand he learned
as a colt, gravity then pulling less
against him.
          Like two helpless sailors
marooned with age, and mourning
a familiar orca beached
in the storm's debris, we crutch
our feeble human frames
beneath the horse's weight and heave
each time he tries. The Rockies return
our holler in a salvo of shouts,
grandstand uproar
we hope will spring him
to his feet. We pack-in water, last-meal

grain and pellets. No way can we swallow easy
looking into the white of a single eye
sinking, giving in to red. No way
hunters can repent—can we take back the metal,
aimed or stray, sent through flesh.
                              Riflefire
across this big-game state
echoes reports of 44 wars
from guerrilla worlds, the unarmed falling
fair prey as varmint, as target,
when killing comes
nonchalant. What's one shot more—mercy
or otherwise—one more animal soul
to this planetful of procreating shots
and souls.
                    Yearlings gallop a kettledrum
roll along the rim. What I can say
in light of this violent world, I hold
silent: Staircase, number 12,
bucker who broke my partner's neck in '78,
who flung me off 3 times
to hometown fans, I wanted this
life of ours—love for what hurt us most—
to last a full, eternal, 8 seconds more.

For Joe Podgurski

Holts

Fittin' a Ride!

The Heavyweight Champion Pie-Eatin' Cowboy of the West

I just ate 50 pies—started off with coconut
macaroon, wedged my way through bar angel
chocolate, Marlborough, black walnut and sour cream
raisin to confetti-crusted crab apple—
still got room for dessert
and they can stick their J-E-L-L-O
where the cowpie don't shine, cause Sugar Plum
I don't eat nothing made from horses' hooves!

So make it something **pie**, something light
and fancy, like huckleberry fluffy chiffon, go
extra heavy on the hucks and fluff—beaten
eggwhites folded in **just** so. Or let's shoot
for something in plaid, red and tan lattice-
topped raspberry, honeyed crust
flakey and blistered to a luster, wild
fruit oozing with a scoop of hard vanilla!

Or maybe I'll strap on a feedbag of something
a smidgen more timid: quivering
custard with its nutmeg-freckled fill
nervous in the shell. Come to think of it now,
blue ribbon mincemeat sounds a lot

more my cut: neck of venison, beef suet,
raisins, apples, citrus peel, currants—
all laced, Grammy-fashion, in blackstrap molasses!

No. Truth is, I'm craving shoofly or spiced rhubarb
or sure hard to match peachy praline,
cinnamon winesap apple à la mode, walnut
crumb or chocolate-frosted pecan. **OR**,
whitecapped high above its fluted deep-dish crust,
a lemon angel meringue—not to mention
mandarin apricot, black bottom, banana cream,
burgundy berry or Bavarian nectarine ambrosia!

And how could you out-gun the Turkeyday
old reliables: sweet potato, its cousin
pumpkin, its sidekicks Dutch apple and cranberry
ice cream nut. Ah, harvest moon, that autumn
gourmet cheese supreme, or Jack Frost squash, or …
"my favorite," you ask? That's a tough one.
Just surprise me with something new, Sweetie
Pie—like tangerine boomerang gooseberry!

FOR LARRY, CURT, JOEL,
JIM AND BUGS

41

In the Money

The Night the Devil Danced on Me

A werewolf moon glares
from the top row of bleachers, horned
        owl with one eye plucked. In the black hole
of chute 8, Lonewolf waits—
        an ugly bronc, mustang and rank,
the cowboys say, with notched right ear
        and snaky, suck-back ways.

        When a sluggish Montana sun goes down,
the crowd packs home its cheers, the screak
        of warm rosin and rawhide
echoes in the arena, and nostrils
        bellow the horse's hot snort. I crack-back
my hand in the riggin', the binds locking
        with a squawk, the bronc coiling below me.

        Above the chute, a jury of broken cowboys
against dusk, silhouettes of crooked limbs
        in an old orchard, and heartwood faces
that stare, like kids look into the gullet
        of a homestead well. I call for the gate,
hinges shriek, sand hisses against the chutes
        with every kick—moons dive in a dirty sky.

        Lonewolf hurls me down
to his farrago of shadows. I'm hung, prey
        under the belly, swung in a fury
of hooves and spurs—claws in the dark:
        ground is a black thunder cloud
and my chaps swoop around me
        like huge wings of a hungry bird.

Dear Mom

"Please don't tell my mother
I'm a rodeo cowboy. She thinks I play
piano at the whorehouse in Wallace, Idaho."

The night that devil danced on me
I know how you barely peeked
between fingers and beads. You heard
the hard blow-by-blow
announcer cawing from the crow's-nest,
above the cowboy holler and dusk,
how I was hung and being drug
by a bronc no one could stop. No,
dad should ***not*** have brought his gun,
and I doubt your rosary
will salvage me from hell. You bet
I can remember
how you massaged my gums
with homemade hootch
to ease the teething,
how you never dreamed
that twenty-three years later
a palomino bronc named Moonshine
would leave me toothless in Missoula.

She Holds Her Favorite Cowboy Close

        Wristwatch strapped over his cuff, a hand
thick as a tractor manifold
        pivots off his daughter's shoulder, his arm
looped around her with savvy
        he's used to slip bridles
on 45 years of colts—"*easy* now"—
        as not to spook a single curl
tumbling beneath the powder-blue Resistol—
        "*easy* now"—as not to foul with diesel or grease,
or the smell of hooves he's just shod,
        her cotton boot-length dress, her satin sash
embossed in silver. She's the crowned
        queen and sweetheart of the "Fremont County Fair
& Rodeo." No mimicked cowboy myth
        posed against their yard fence,
the burrowings of bark beetles in slab
        pickets like swivel-cut leather—
against spirited horses grazing
        blurred acres beyond the camera's depth of field.
No fat or phony frills taint this span
        of father-daughter, lean grin and wide smile
matching perfectly the casts
        of their trophy buckles beaming side by side,
and the speckle-faced Aussie cowdog, squatting
        perk-eared and cocked for some action he craves
outside this frame. The West before wire
        still rides the lineage of this family ranch
where broncs, pastured with the bridlewise,
        fashion a soft backdrop for lovers
of horses—like father, like daughter—
        blue-ribboned in their Wind River embrace.

For Cathy Griffin Jacobson & The Mantle Family

Samurai Cowboy

Hung over from pitchers of Margaritas,
Chimayo cocktails, and crockery cruets of hot saki,
the samurai cowboy rises early and drinks
a cowcamp potful of Guatemalan roast
to Ian Tyson singing "Gallo de Cielo." He loves
this ballad of the gladiator rooster of heaven,
its heart for the battle, and how,
"facing the wicked black, it sinks
a gaff into Zorro's shiny breast."
He loves how they collide and lift
into a twister of wings, beaks, claws and squawks
37 times, like rounds between bare-knucklers,
till Gallo de Cielo's valiant death. He allows
how it's the lilt and lingo, the dance,
the passion that makes this song
his anthem. Riding or writing,
poem or rodeo, he craves the heart-pummeling,
liver-risking, soul-staking physical.

She, in black kimono, serenely irons
the denim dress she'll wear to work
in Santa Fe with snakeskin, lavender,
scallop-top Tony Lamas. She basks in
the decor of her adobe-lodgepole house,
a collage of trappings, art, and kitsch—
the Orient with cowboy West—

of braided rawhide reatas, of soft
McCarty woven from mane hair, of Hopi baskets
from banana yucca, of origami, and horse clocks,
Navajo rugs, kachina and kokeshi dolls,
of bonsai and sprigs of silk cherry blossoms,
peyote buttons to fend off pesky spirits,
cholla skeleton and bamboo furniture, Zuni fetish,
and kamikaze kite. She irons with a grin,
watching him strut and fly
on adrenalined memories of old broncs
and new love, on caffeine and fiery lyrics.

He paces, in the living room, his pre-ride
ritual behind the chutes. He slashes
spurstrokes in his stockinged feet, left
then right, his high-stepping samurai stride,
dexterous as a cricket, toes turned out,
heels gripping against the shock-
tremor of the bronc's shoulders. He holds
his free hand high, his riding arm flexed,
fist clenched, against his trophy buckle,
to an imaginary bareback riggin', his teeth clamped,
spitfire through the slits of his eyes
as he slashes and slashes: the rodeo poet—
only a skosh mad from living too long
alone to spur the broncs—gassing it
from Missoula to Tesuque
in his antique cowboy cadillac
to cross pastoral Japanese with roughstock sonnet
with love for the geisha cowgal in blond.

Hang and Drag

Hang and Drag No. 2

Heading Home

THE COMEBACK

Too stove-up most nights to sleep,
he sprawls on a sway-backed sofa
and entertains his pain with pulp westerns,
pages canted toward the white light of a t.v.
gone hours ago to snow, the squelch
tuned low to drown the humdrum of his pulse.

At his feet, a bareback riggin' is set
to the withers-thick arm of the couch. It perches
like an idol, a bird of prey
with its head—the handhold—wedged
between hunch-shouldered wings—the fringed black
chaps draped over it like a shawl.

The man's eyes burning, words gone blurred,
soon the book gables his sternum
and he stares through it to the rowel-
notched surcingle. He resurrects each bronc
that bucked, in 8 ticks, a year's worth of grit,
till his spur-lick lifts him through the flying

change from wakefulness to dreams
obsessed. The spasms in his back
prod his squirming to a toss
and roll—a horse quelling its lathered itch—
couch springs as raucous
as that squawk of the gut at a trot.

First bars of the channel's 6 a.m. anthem
lap with dream and touch
his nerves off like fuses in the chute. He rises,
steps into a hackney-ride day
between comebacks, weathers one more
long go-'round of seconds too tame to count.

FOR RED SHUTTLEWORTH

Moonshine

You've heard of Kessler's Blended Whiskey—
that silk-smooth spur juice don't bite or snort or kick at all.
    With 3-fingers' mane-holt to a jigger glass
I've rode amber bottles to an empty standstill,
        fanned 'em for the crowd at closing time,
catapulted off the barstool and never took a fall.

But have you heard of Kesler's "Moonshine?"
That's Reg, **MISTER** Rodeo, Kesler, spelled with just one s.
    And though we're talkin' buckin' horse, not hootch,
that 1200 proof of palomino lightning
        turned a boastful headstrong twister
to a puny, knee-walkin', toilet-huggin' punch-drunk mess.

That gelding seldom changed his gameplan.
He sort of drifted left with lots of drop and hell for stout.
    In the chute, his dude-horse nonchalance
made you crave coffee and a quirly,
        till he squatted to the gatelatch rattle,
a cocked, hair-triggered set-gun, deadly for that first jump out.

Moonshine led his champion band of bares,
the blue norther's fury from Canada to Spanish lands.
    With Three Bars, Applejack, and Creamo,
they bucked their famous raindance

when riggin' riders shook their faces,
and arenas took a pelting from downpours of top hands.

That day "Wolf" Loney drawed him down at Dillon,
I slowly shouldered next to Reg and heard his whispered cheers.
   "Come on, Yeller. Come **ON**, Yeller,"
as Moonshine cracked 'em harder
   to win that bout in seven—
through Reg's grit and rawhide squint, the gleam of prideful tears.

Because rodeo means partnership with passion—
legacies of beautiful duets, loves you'll never lose.
   I still believed in Santa Claus and comebacks
when down in Santa Fe I read
   "Moonshine put to sleep at 33"—
I toasted Reg and Yeller with a jug of homemade booze.

That night, bucked off hard and whiskey dreaming,
I'm entered-up in seventh heaven, free of age and pain.
   Cy's voice raves "number 33 with Kesler"
as they float out like gliding
   ballroom stars—Reg, grinning,
waltzing close, holding gently on to Moonshine's golden mane.

MEASURING

Maybe today she'll know me,
the alfalfa, brome, timothy, and horse
aroma I track in with a limp
to this rest home. Thrown again,
rodeo-old at 30, I visit her, a pioneer
schoolmarm excused from the world
she risked 90 years. Her skin,
fragile as frostbitten leaf,
flinches to the cold touch
of a hot-fudge shake, a favorite
treat I hope will soothe
her scorn for the nightmare fate
she wakes to. She scans this one-room life
in silence, eyes still keen to a horse or boy
who favors one leg. She recites my name,
poised like a pupil answering right,
and then, in slow soliloquy
between sips of chocolate, a child's voice
warns how pain gone dormant wakes
all at once.
                    Through window film
thick as cataracts, I fix
on aspen turning yellow,
in the green world of fir,
after autumn frost. Children spring up

like a fairy ring—one quick blink—all spunk
from the monkey bars next door. They swing,
teeter, and flip
gymnastic routines to the beat
of laughter and brabble
vanishing into back yards
and vacant lots.
     Watching me
watch those children, maybe
she remembers the way memory was
once an easy measure, a finger count,
simple as that certain space
for love—***This much***—we clung to
like a fantasy, a mirage—youth
secure between arms flung wide.

Digging In

Riding In His Mind

Zarzyski Stomachs the Oxford Special with Zimmer at the Ox Bar & Grill

Donning his bronc-stomper black hat, cock-eyed
the morning after reading range rhymes
in Montana, Zimmer swears out loud
his belly's tough as whang leather,
reckons his grease count's a skosh low,
and it behooves us, here in cattleland,
to brunch on cow—no quiche,
no veggie omelet or henfruit Benedict
when Zimmer's craving beeve, a hoof-'n'-horn
dogie-puncher dose of B-12
to prod toward procreation
two braincells the whiskey failed to pickle.

Zarzyski thinks Zimmer figures
rare steak and eggs a pair
till he catches Zimmer's eyes, ruminating
behind the stained menu—that devious gleam.
Zimmer has brains on the mind.

Zimmer has brains on his mind
and Zarzyski knows too well The Zimmer Dictum:
what suits one P.Z., damned straight tickles
another P.Z. plum pink. Sure as shit
and shootin', like a gunslinger
demanding redeye, crusty-throated Zimmer hollers
"Bring us hombres brains and eggs."
And the waitress relays Zimmer's whimsy
to a fry-cook big enough to eat hay
and dirty-up the floor. In short-order lingo
she yells, "these boys **need em**, Sam—
these Z-boys **need em** real awful bad."

CALL ME LUCKY

      She eases the silver barrette
from her palomino hair,
      one long strand still clinging,
and hands it to me
      for good luck. I've tried everything
from striped socks to homespun prayer—
      even had the lining in my hat signed
by a famous country-western singer
      cooing in her long southern drawl,
"hold on *real* tight now." Still
      those broncs keep dumping me,
Stetson-first, into arena
      after arena dirt and fences.
Somebody up there loves bucking
      horses more than me, and nothing
but nothing's going to change that—unless
      maybe this silver barrette
from a girl raised with a mustang
      Montana wind in her mane.

THE BUCKING HORSE MOON

A kiss for luck, then we'd let 'er buck—
I'd spur electric on adrenaline and lust.
      She'd figure-8 those barrels
on her Crimson Missile sorrel—
      we'd make the night air swirl with hair and dust.

At some sagebrushed wayside, 3 a.m.,
we'd water, grain, and ground-tie Missile.
      Zip our sleeping bags together,
make love in any weather,
      amid the cactus, rattlers, and thistle.

Seems the moon was always full for us—
its high-diving shadow kicking hard.
      We'd play kid games on the big night sky,
she'd say "that bronco's Blue-Tail Fly,
      and ain't that ol' J.T. spurrin' off its stars?"

We knew sweet youth's no easy keeper.
It's spent like winnings, all too soon.
      So we'd revel every minute
in the music of our Buick
      running smooth, two rodeoin' lovers
cruising to another—
      beneath Montana's blue roan
bucking horse moon.

The Augusta perf at 2, we'd place again,
then sneak off to our secret Dearborn River spot.
    We'd take some chips and beer and cheese,
skinny-dip, dry off in the breeze,
      build a fire, fry the trout we caught.

    Down moonlit gravel back to blacktop,
she'd laugh and kill those beams for fun.
    That old wagon road was ours to own—
30 shows since I'd been thrown
      and 87 barrels since she'd tipped one.

    We knew that youth won't keep for rainy days.
It burns and turns to ash too soon.
    So we'd revel every minute
in the music of our Buick
      running smooth, two rodeoin' lovers
cruising to another—
      beneath Montana's blue roan
bucking horse moon.

Afternoon Shadows